Alien
Adventures

Pit-stop
Peril

James Noble • Jonatror˙

OXFORD
UNIVERSITY PRESS

Max's mission log

We are travelling through space on board the micro-ship Excelsa with our new friend, Eight.

We are trying to get home. Our only chance is to get to the Waythroo Wormhole — a space tunnel that should lead us back to our own galaxy. We don't have long. The wormhole is due to collapse very soon. If we don't get there in time, we'll be trapped in the Delta-Zimmer Galaxy forever!

To make matters worse, a space villain called Badlaw is following us in his Destroyer ship. Badlaw and his army of robotic Krools want to take over Earth. We can't let that happen!

Our new mission is simple: to shake off Badlaw and get to the Waythroo Wormhole before it collapses. I just wish it was as easy as it sounds.

Time until wormhole collapses: 3 days, I hour and 9 minutes

In our last adventure ...

We were on our way to the Waythroo Wormhole when we came across a giant patch of mist. A huge eye appeared in the middle of it. The mist was a rust monster called Rustan! We tried to escape but Rustan touched the Excelsa, which immediately started to rust.

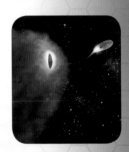

We headed to the nearest planet (Mechio) to repair our ship, but soon realized that Rustan had followed us. The Mechions agreed to help us even though they knew Rustan could destroy their metallic planet.

Ant had an idea to help save the Mechions from the rust monster. Eight built a giant magnetic wave-blaster and we used magnetic dust to push Rustan back out into space.

Chapter 1 – Tracked down

Cat sat forward in her chair, peering anxiously at the screen on her desk.

"There's something following us," she said, "and it's catching up."

The friends gathered round the screen and watched a flashing dot on the monitor. It was flying fast and heading straight for the Excelsa.

"*WARNING*," said the ship. "*Long-range tracer dart detected.*"

Eight gave a worried bleep and plugged into Cat's desk.

"The signal shows that it is coming from the Destroyer," she said.

"Badlaw must have programmed it to find us so he can track us down," said Ant.

"I'll try to lose it!" Tiger called from the pilot's seat. He pushed hard on the steering orbs, turning the ship sharply.

"It's not working – it's still gaining on us!" cried Cat. She watched as the tracer dart got closer and closer.

Ant ran to his desk and pushed a lever to increase the ship's speed. The Excelsa shot forward, but the tracer dart followed their every move.

Red warning lights flashed and a loud alarm wailed.

"***DANGER! Tracer dart within range***," said the ship.

Cat watched her screen in horror as the tracer dart flew in a fast circle around the Excelsa. Then there was a loud *THUD*. The ship rocked as the dart planted itself firmly on the hull.

"***Tracer dart attached***," the ship said. "***We are now being tracked***."

Chapter 2 – Diversion

Max hurried towards the main door. "We need to get outside and remove that dart. Who's coming to help?"

"That will not work," said Eight. "Tracer darts cannot simply be pulled off."

"We need to get rid of it somehow," insisted Tiger. "We can't head home if Badlaw's tracking us."

The crew were on their way to the Waythroo Wormhole. They hoped it would take them back to their home galaxy. Badlaw had been following them hoping to get to Earth, and the last thing they wanted to do was lead him straight there.

"Cat, please set a course for the Glimstar Quadrant," bleeped Eight. "We need to make a bit of a detour."

Cat looked nervous. "Why? What's there?"

"A space garage," said Eight. "There may be a mechanic there who can help us remove the tracer dart."

"We must be quick," said Max. "Badlaw won't waste any time hunting us down now."

"And we've only got three days to get to the wormhole," Tiger added.

Chapter 3 – The space garage

It wasn't long before the friends saw the space garage come into view. There was a line of floating spaceships trailing from the garage.

"Look at the queue!" wailed Cat. "Badlaw will have caught up with us long before we reach the front of that lot."

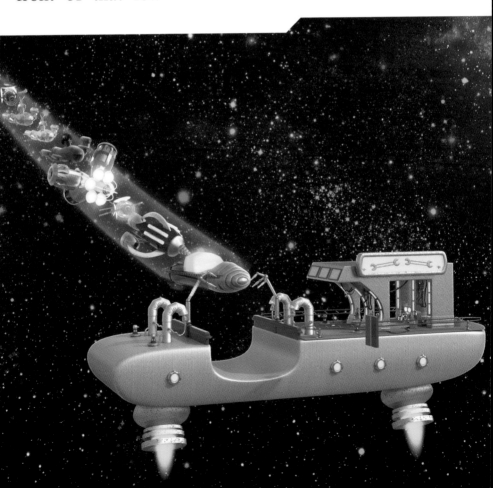

"Tiger, take us to the front of the queue," said Max. "Let's find out what's causing the hold-up. Maybe there's something we can do to help get this lot moving."

Tiger guided the micro-ship through the traffic. None of the other ships seemed to mind as he weaved between them, getting closer and closer to the front of the line.

They soon reached the garage. Tiger brought the Excelsa in to land.

"Nice flying, Tiger," said Ant, as they made their way to the hold.

"Fix your helmets and set your gravity boots to maximum," said Max. When they had done as he asked, Max opened the exit hatch, pushed a button and lowered the holo-ramp.

Space garages

Like vehicles on Earth, all spaceships need maintenance and servicing. There is a network of space garages across the universe where intergalactic travellers can stop to refuel or to have repair work carried out.

Services offered

▶ Refuelling
▶ Repairs
▶ Cleaning
▶ Servicing

Number of garages

There are over 10,000 space garages in the Delta-Zimmer Galaxy alone.

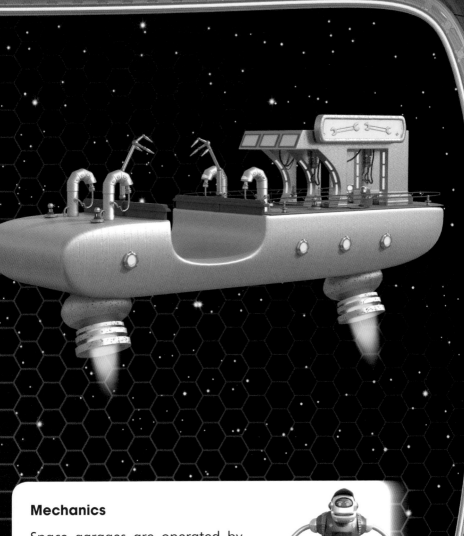

Mechanics

Space garages are operated by droids specially programmed to repair any model of spaceship. They are extremely helpful and efficient.

Once they were clear of the micro-ship, the friends pressed their buttons and grew to normal size.

"That's strange," said Tiger. He paused and listened hard. It was eerily quiet. "All the spaceships in that queue are silent."

"Their engines are probably just switched off," said Ant, looking around the garage.

Just then a small, red droid whizzed up to them. It had silver mechanical legs and three wheels instead of feet.

Max stepped forwards. "That's the longest queue I've ever seen for a garage," he said, pointing towards the line of spaceships. "Is everything OK?"

The droid didn't reply. Instead, his eyes flashed different colours as he scanned the children. Cat thought he seemed on edge, but with a long line of customers it was understandable, wasn't it?

When the droid spoke, his voice was loud and rough. "I have so much work to do. I can't fix this many ships by myself." The droid looked helplessly at the long queue.

"Maybe we can help?" said Ant.

"Really?" said the robot, looking relieved. "I would be very grateful."

"If we help you," said Max, "could you help us in return by removing a tracer dart from our ship?"

"Of course, I'd be happy to," replied the droid enthusiastically.

"Max," Cat said urgently, "Badlaw will be here soon. I really don't think we've got time to help repair all those spaceships."

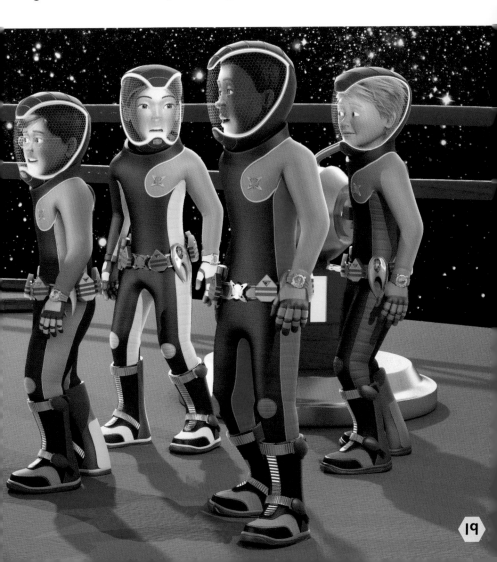

"With your help, I'm sure it won't take very long," the droid said. "As for that tracer dart, I've got a special device that will have it off in no time."

"Great, let's get started then," said Max. "The sooner we get your jobs done, the sooner we can get on our way."

Chapter 4 – A helping hand

"First things first," said the droid. "I'm Moki." He extended a robotic arm, as if to shake Max's hand.

Max hesitated. Moki didn't have a hand – he had a red hammer.

"Oops!" said Moki. "I'm a repair droid. I know I have hands somewhere …"

"We don't have to shake hands," said Max. "Let's get to work."

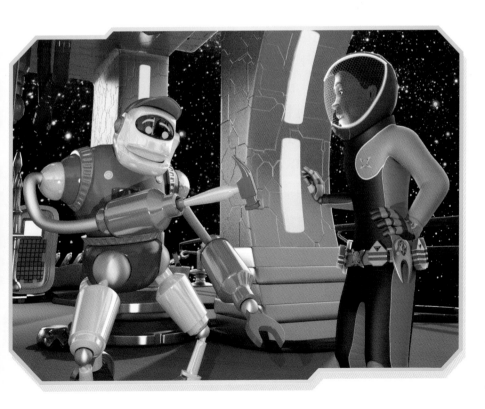

The repair droid made his way over to a large, red hover-bike.

"My bike is broken. Without it, I can't get around to service the ships quickly. If you could fix it for me, I could get round to all the customers in this queue in no time."

"No problem," said Tiger. "I'm good with machines. I can usually figure them out!"

Tiger borrowed a set of tools from Moki and walked over to the bike.

He climbed on it and pressed the starter button. The machine choked and coughed but it wouldn't start. He took out a spanner from a nearby toolbox and opened the control panel. Then he shrank to micro-size so that he could get a closer look at the bike's wiring and set to work.

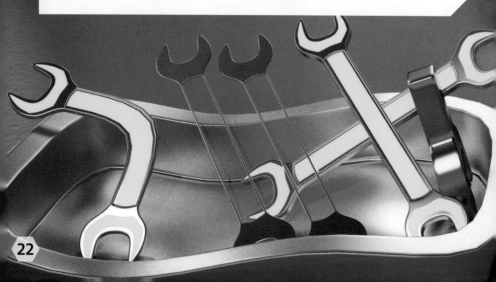

"While Tiger's fixing your bike, could we make a start on removing that dart?" Cat asked Moki.

"Actually, that fuel pump is broken," said Moki. "Could you have a look at it? I'm sure it won't take long."

"I'll take a look," said Ant, heading across the garage.

Ant looked at the pump. The fuel indicator was on zero. He walked round the other side of the pump. There was a metallic hose lying on the floor. Ant knelt down and inspected it. "*Hey*," he said to himself. "*This pump's not broken ... it's just been disconnected.*"

Ant reconnected the hose and tightened the clamp to hold it in place. Immediately the fuel indicator lit up.

Chapter 5 – No more delays

Ant returned to his friends on the other side of the garage. Cat and Eight were helping Moki repair the docking clamps, and Max was sweeping the space dust away from the docking bay. He looked up as Ant approached.

"Max, I've got a funny feeling about this place," said Ant.

"What do you mean?" asked Max.

"Something's not right …"

Before he could explain, Ant was cut off by the roar of the hover-bike.

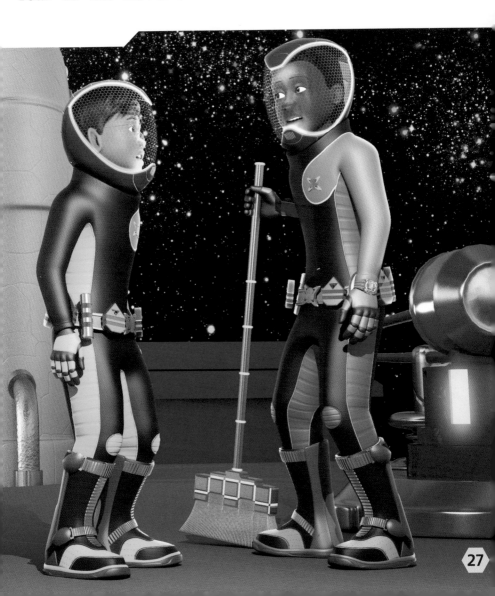

The brakes screeched as Tiger came in to land. He skidded to a halt.

"You've fixed it!" Max said. "Well done, Tiger."

"Easy peasy, there were just a couple of loose connections," said Tiger, climbing off the bike to join the others.

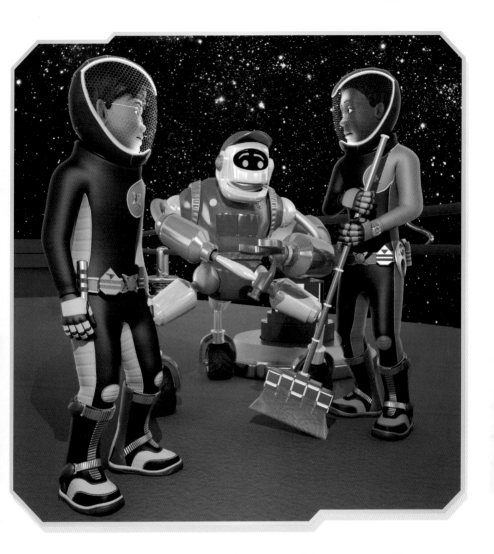

Max turned to the droid. "Moki, we really need to get going. Now will you help us?"

"Yes, of course I will," said Moki. "There's just one more thing. All these broken old spaceships passing through have made my gravity flooring very dirty. It could really do with a clean."

"But I've swept it already," said Max.

"It needs washing and polishing, too. The dirt is making the gravity magnets weak, but they can easily be restored … with your help," said Moki.

"Does it really need to be done right now?" asked Tiger impatiently.

"It would be a real help!" Moki bleeped, whizzing over to collect some mops.

Max sighed. "OK, but this will have to be the very last thing. After we've done this, will you please help us with our ship?"

"That's my next job. Promise," replied Moki, with a nervous grin.

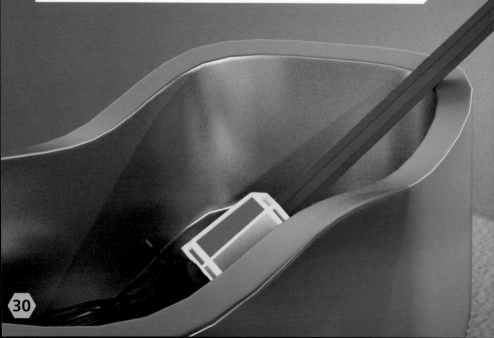

"Max, we really don't have time," Ant pleaded. "It's OK, Ant," said Max. "I know how we can get this done quickly." He pressed the button on his suit and wings slid out from his back.

Max took a mop from Moki and rose into the air. Then he zoomed across the garage with the mop, leaving a gleaming trail behind him.

The others quickly followed him. In no time, the gravity flooring was sparkling clean.

Cat turned to Moki. "Tiger's fixed your hover-bike, Ant's fixed the fuel pump, Eight and I have helped you repair the docking clamps, and we've all helped you clean your floor. Now can you help us fix our ship?"

Moki looked around the garage again.

"Moki!" said Max. "We need your help, now!"

"OK, OK," Moki bleeped and sighed. "I'll do it."

Moki rummaged through a large toolbox. A moment later, he pulled out a claw-shaped device which he quickly attached to his arm. Then he headed for the micro-ship.

The tracer dart was sticking out from the back, near the rear power cells. The clamp at the end of it was firmly attached to the hull.

"Nasty little things, tracer darts. Very tricky to remove if you don't know what you are doing," Moki said, as he reached for the dart. "It's a 648 ... a particularly advanced model ... very precise tracking functions."

"That's why we need to get out of here. Badlaw will know exactly where we are by now," Cat said.

Moki began to shake.

Moki clamped the pincers around the head of the dart and turned the claw three times. The dart came free with a loud *POP!*

"There you go, one tracer dart removed," said Moki. "I'll get rid of this for you."

"Thank you. Now we should really ..." Max was suddenly interrupted by a rumbling sound. The garage started to shake and the floor trembled.

"What's going on?" cried Cat.

Chapter 6 – Badlaw's attack

The friends turned to see Badlaw's Destroyer ship in the distance, heading for the space garage.

Just then, the spaceships in the queue started to flicker. Some of them disappeared completely!

"Look!" Tiger yelled. "They're not real. Those spaceships are just holograms!"

"We've been tricked," said Cat angrily.

They all turned to Moki.

"You tricked us!" said Max. "You didn't need our help at all."

Moki's eyes flickered and his screen flushed a hot, red colour. He looked at the floor sadly. "I am sorry. I had no choice."

"What do you mean?" asked Ant.

"I received a message from Badlaw," explained Moki. "He said that I had to lay a trap for some space-travellers who might be heading my way. If I didn't help him, he said he would blow my garage to smithereens!"

Cat shook her fists. "That sneaky alien," she growled.

"We need to do something," said Ant. "And fast!"

Badlaw was flying through the line of holograms, getting closer and closer to the garage all the time.

"I am sorry that I tricked you," Moki said. "I realize now that you are brave and kind. I must be brave like you. Please, take your spaceship and fly away from here. I will wait for Badlaw."

"We can't leave," said Ant. "Badlaw will destroy your garage if you let us go."

"Do not worry," Moki said. "I have an idea."

"You are brave, Moki," said Cat. "Thank you and good luck!"

The friends shrank and ran towards the Excelsa.

Chapter 7 – Escaping Badlaw

The crew took their places back on board the micro-ship.

"Let's get out of here," said Max.

Tiger pulled the steering orbs and the ship blasted off. Seconds later, Badlaw's Destroyer arrived and hovered over Moki's garage.

"Let's hope Moki's plan works," said Cat.

"Ant, increase acceleration," Max said.

"Wait!" Cat said suddenly. "There's something on my screen ..." As she studied her monitor, lots of dots began to appear one after the other. "Ships!" she exclaimed. "Hundreds of them."

"Not just any ship ..." said Max, looking out of the viewscreen.

Surrounding the micro-ship were lots of identical Excelsas.

Ant grinned. "They're holograms! Moki's made copies of our ship. Badlaw won't know which of us to chase."

Suddenly, the Destroyer appeared ahead of them. Together, all the Excelsas lurched to a stop as they came head-to-head with their enemy.

Badlaw's angry face appeared on the Excelsa's viewscreen.

"Those hologram images won't last for long," Badlaw's voice boomed. "I've got all the time in the universe to wait for them to disappear ..."

"Ah! It seems that I don't even have to wait! My scanners have just detected a signal from my tracer dart," Badlaw continued. "Now I have you!" The screen flickered and went blank.

Max looked at his friends with horror. "He can't have. Moki said he would get rid of it."

"Unless Moki's changed his mind about helping us and wants to save his garage after all," said Tiger.

"Or maybe Moki's got another surprise for us," said Cat, pointing to her screen. "There's the tracer dart, and it's heading in the opposite direction to us."

Little did Badlaw know that Moki had attached the dart to his newly-repaired hover-bike, which was now heading far off into the Delta-Zimmer Galaxy.

"We'll be far away from here before Badlaw realizes it's a trick," said Tiger.

The holograms of the Excelsa gradually started to fade and disappear. The real Excelsa zoomed off, leaving the space garage and Badlaw far behind.

Find out what happens next in *The Red Cutlass.*

The Red Cutlass